MAY YOUR SPIRIT BE uplifted ♡

Loretta Wood Nevez

Refreshment for the Caregiver's Spirit

LORETTA WOODWARD VENEY

INFINITY
PUBLISHING

ISBN 978-1-4958-1374-0
ISBN 978-1-4958-1375-7 eBook
Library of Congress Control Number: 2017903664

Published April 2017

INFINITY PUBLISHING
1094 New DeHaven Street, Suite 100
West Conshohocken, PA 19428-2713
Toll-free (877) BUY BOOK
Local Phone (610) 941-9999
Fax (610) 941-9959
Info@buybooksontheweb.com
www.buybooksontheweb.com

Contents

Dedication

I dedicate this book to Timothy MacBeth Veney, my biggest cheerleader, best friend of 36 years, soulmate and husband of almost 31 years. This book wouldn't be possible without the amazing photos he took on our many travels and adventures. Tim loved life and lived it to the fullest each and every day. He had a magnetic smile and captivating laugh and impacted the lives of everyone around him.

Tim made you feel special even if you only met him once, and he made my Mom feel special on each and every visit, even after she no longer remembered who we were. When I became an author as part of my fight against Alzheimer's disease, Tim was with me every step of the way. He packed and mailed books all around the country, and entertained folks standing in line at my book signings. Tim knew I was working on this book to lift the spirits of Caregivers, and he was thrilled that some of his favorite photos would become part of the book. I'm devastated that he died after a very short illness on July 17, 2016, but he lives on in the lives of all of us who knew and loved him.

Tim, Thank you for loving me and for always holding me up!

I miss you every day and will love you always!

Cover photo: Naples, Italy © Tim Veney, 2016

Update on Being My Mom's Mom

My first book, Being My Mom's Mom was published on February 1, 2013. The last few lines of the book are "For the rest of her life, I will ensure she gets exactly what she wants, because she gave birth to me and I love her with all my heart. While I was never blessed with having children of my own, God has entrusted me with being my Mom's mom. No matter what awaits me and my Mom in the future, I pray that I'll continue to have the love, strength and courage to be the best Mom for her I can be."

To date, I'm living up to the promise I made at the end of the book. Mom's physical health is still quite good, really amazing for an 88 year-old woman, but her dementia has progressed significantly. The journey has by no means been easy. Dementia is a "take one day at a time" type of disease, and every single day is different.

I'm very proud of all the incredible things that have occurred since Being My Mom's Mom was published, and Mom would be very proud if she understood. I've been on an amazing book tour thanks to Julie Boone Roth, the amazing Marketing Director at the Silver Spring, Maryland location of Arden Courts Memory Care Community (a division of HCR-ManorCare Nursing Homes). Julie and I were both vendors at an Active Aging Conference in Maryland in May of 2013 when I walked over to her table and gave her a signed copy of my book, primarily because I didn't want to carry all the books back home that I had brought with me. A few days later, Julie emailed me to say she was really enjoying the book and wanted me to speak at her facility in the fall. I was thrilled, and the November 2013 event was my first speaking gig outside of a book signing at my church and friends and family gatherings. At Julie's request, I sent ten books to HCR-ManorCare management to determine if my book would be housed in their warehouse. Amazingly, the book was accepted and I began working with HCR-ManorCare marketing communication director Kelly Lippincott who scheduled me to speak at many Arden Courts locations throughout the country. Those speaking and book signing events have been some of the most exciting times of my life.

During the three years of speaking engagements thus far, I've met people with whom I'll be friends for the rest of my life! I've signed autographs in addition to books, and have been treated like royalty. In addition to my speaking fee, some of the locations have given me incredibly thoughtful gifts, such as tea cups, a teddy bear crocheted by a church's Alzheimer's ministry, writing journals, caregiver notebooks, pens and even spa baskets. I've also done a lot of work with the Central and Western Virginia Chapter of the Alzheimer's Association working with Ellen Phipps, and the National Capital Area Chapter, working with Linda Williams. The experience and information I've received has prepared me to be as knowledgeable as possible whenever I speak. In the last year, I've had the honor of working with Amy DePreker of Artis Senior Living and Pat O'Connor of Brookdale Senior Living, Inc. Speaking at these memory care facilities has been incredible!. I've also given presentations to support groups, book clubs, sororities, churches and a few chapters of AARP.

One of the most exciting occurrences was Mom and I being featured in a Washington Post article written by my friend Kristen Hartke that was published on July 19th, two days after Tim's death. Tim had threatened to buy 100 copies of the article, and I was happy that he at least got to hear about the interviews I did with Kristen and he was there for the photo shoot with photographer Linda Davidson.

We were also featured in a PBS documentary that was filmed in April of 2016. Senior Producer / Director Mason Mills interviewed me twice. Once in Danville, VA after a presentation for the Alzheimer's Association and the other a few weeks later when Mason came to our home. Tim fixed an excellent dinner and Mason ate with us. He loved the time he had to spend with Mom and me, and with Tim. Mason asked if he could add a special dedication to Tim at end the film when it released in November 2016, and of course I said yes. The episode aired in the Richmond, VA area on November 10th and was live streamed on Facebook. Not only was there a special dedication to Tim at the end of the documentary, he was also featured in a scene assisting Mom getting in our vehicle, which was incredible because it truly showed Tim's love for Mom.

Being My Mom's Mom was based on six elements. What follows is an update in each of the areas since 2013.

FORGIVENESS

Forgiving ourselves is almost a daily requirement when you're caring for someone with dementia. There are days that we just aren't going to be happy with how things work out. We will feel guilty about the things we did or didn't do. We will be disappointed with others who say they will help or provides services, but never follow through. I have had to forgive myself for the guilt around the fact that there are days that I find it difficult to spend a lot of time with Mom. I love seeing her, because though she no longer knows who I am, whenever she sees me she says "HI" with the most energizing enthusiasm you can imagine. We always hug too, which is also very special because Mom was never a big hugger when we were growing up. My typical visit with Mom is to sit with her and address what's happening at that moment – the weather, what she's reading, what's coming up on the calendar – holidays etc. That usually takes all of 15 minutes. After that, the visit gets a little uncomfortable at times. Mom asks me what I'm doing there, then I pretend to be whomever she believes I am at that moment (usually not a relative I know that well). That takes another 5 minutes or so. Then I usually get my phone out and flip through the old photos as Mom names everyone in the photos (as long as the picture is pre-1950). Mom still loves to read and I'm grateful that she can still do so. However, the reading material is usually something very generic, like a two-year old Reader's Digest and nothing about current events because that causes her more confusion than enjoyment. There are times that Mom will read to me and sometimes I read to her. Though it's nothing too exciting, us reading together keeps us engaged. She also really likes looking at the pictures in the magazines and comments on what the people are wearing because she isn't up on current fashion styles. I cherish these moments because I know it won't be long before she no longer remembers how to read. Starting on Thanksgiving Day of 2016, I tried coloring with Mom and she loved it! She didn't finish the one page she colored, but she was very proud of her art work. The coloring continued on Christmas day too and kept her very entertained.

More than anything, I miss talking about our lives and having meaningful conversation. Usually after forty-five minutes or so of activity, it's usually time for me to go, or we sit silently until we start the process all over again. It's so hard to stay for several hours at a time, trying to find conversation topics and some days it's easier than others. Thankfully, when I take her out we spend a lot more time together because there are many things for her to see, do and focus on. She loves riding in the car and looking out the window, something she absolutely hated to do when I was a kid. In spite of the unpredictable things that happen, we can't forget to forgive ourselves when we get frustrated, hurt or angry. It all comes with the territory with this disease. Over the past six months or so, I've been really working on just being present with Mom and not having to say or do anything. That has allowed me to significantly increase the time I sit with her.

I also readily practice forgiveness for all the people who typically say or do mean things when Mom and I are out in public. Because she is such a physically healthy person, I make it a point to get her out as often as possible! When we are in line somewhere or walking around, it's amazing the crazy things people say. They'll ask for example "why does she keep saying the same thing?" to whomever they're with. Or they'll say "I wish she'd stop saying that" or worse still, "she's getting on my last nerve." I try to ignore people most of the time, but people can be cruel. I just pray for them and forgive them.

One person I wasn't as able to readily forgive was a neurologist we visited in early 2016. She was one of the neurologists I was "auditioning" to replace Dr. Coerver who relocated to Denver, Colorado in 2015. This doctor failed her audition miserably. First, she made us wait more than an hour before she entered the exam room as if she was doing us a favor. We never waited more than 5 minutes to see Dr. Coerver. After the potential new doctor finally entered the room she came in with the excuse that her staff "didn't tell me you were here". I didn't believe her, and it was an incredible example of throwing your staff under the bus. The same staff that I'm also sure she had charge me $250 for a visit when I had been told that they accepted Medicaid. If those two things weren't enough, what was especially hard for me to forgive was her insensitivity to Mom's disease though she is a neurologist. She asked Mom all the traditional questions, the day, the season and the name of the President of the United States. Mom, of course, didn't know any of the answers. Most doctors move on to the next part of the exam, but not this one. As soon as Mom missed the question about who the President was, the doctor got angry. She told Mom she needed to know who the President was because we were all African-American. What? For just a minute I thought she was kidding, but she absolutely wasn't. I quickly stopped her from chastising Mom by saying. "she doesn't know who I am, how do you expect her to know who President Obama is?". She continued by stating that we need to know our history and I needed to share that information with her so that she remembers. With that statement I gathered up our stuff and Mom and headed out the door, snatching the prescription she was holding in her hand as we left. I was very angry when we left, primarily because as a neurologist, she of all doctors should know how the memory works, or doesn't work with Alzheimer's patients. I forgive her for how she treated Mom, because I walked away from the situation quickly, but I don't forgive her for how she may treat her other patients who don't have someone to advocate for them. Forgiveness is still key!

PATIENCE

One of the questions I get asked most often is about the patience it takes to care for or spend time with someone with dementia. When I'm out with Mom, people often watch us intently because it's obvious after about 2 minutes that Mom has dementia, primarily because of the number of times she repeats the same phrases, questions or sentences. One of the new things she says since the book was published is "I want to go to my other place". That typically means she's out with me at my house or a restaurant and wants to return to the group home where she's very comfortable. I never get upset when she says that because more than anything I want her to be comfortable and anxiety-free.

Easter Egg Hunts – Mom gets distracted very quickly, but it just takes patience to wait for her to calm down. Failing to have patience in certain situations can cause you to miss out on amazing family memories. On Easter of 2014, I picked Mom up and told her we were going to my house for an Easter Egg Hunt with her then 2 year-old great granddaughter Kendal. She immediately got upset, and said she didn't know what Easter was, or what egg hunts were and she didn't want to do it. She then said she wanted to go back to her place. I could have gotten aggravated and just taken her back as she requested. But because we had worked hard setting up the egg hunt, stuffing the plastic eggs with treats and hiding them in the yard, I wanted to at least see if she would give it a try once we got to my house. The experiment went better than we could ever have dreamed. We gave Mom an Easter basket to collect her eggs and pointed she and Kendal to the backyard. At first, Mom said her famous line "I don't know what I'm doing" and Kendal said "come with me Grandma" and Mom followed her. Kendal saw an egg and started to run for it, so Mom ran too. Kendal got to the egg and put it in her basket as Mom watched intently. Mom said, "I see one too". She raced for it, and put it in her basket. Then for about 25 minutes Mom and Kendal ran through our yard finding plastic eggs everywhere and squealing with delight, especially when Mom learned that there was candy or dried fruit in the plastic eggs. We believe that Kendal is one of the kindest kids around and one of the things that made that Easter so memorable was the fact that Kendal made sure to share her eggs with Mom so they'd have an equal amount. After the Easter Egg hunt was over, we went out to the front yard and Mom and Kendal played catch with Kendal's Dora ball. It was so beautiful watching them together that both my daughter and I shed a few tears of joy!

The photos we took of the game of catch were amazing and we will treasure them forever. In our favorite photo, Kendal has her arms outstretched as the ball left her hands, and Mom has her arms out to catch the ball as it comes toward her. Immediately after the visit, Mom had forgotten all about what we had done that afternoon. When I showed her the amazing photo of her hands out to catch the ball, she asked me "did I catch the ball?". When I confirmed that she did, she said "Yay me!" What we didn't realize in that first year was that we started a new and very important tradition. Mom talked quite a bit in 2014, but now talks in just a few words at a time, except to Kendal with whom she will share complete sentences. We've done two more Easter Egg hunts since 2014, and they've both been great successes. They still giggle while they search for eggs, and squeal with delight when they discover which treats are in their eggs, and they still share their eggs and treats. I love the photos we take of Mom and Kendal together, because even though Mom doesn't realize that Kendal is her great-granddaughter, there's an incredible amount of love in the photos.

There have been very few behavioral changes in Mom. She's never had any angry outbursts, but she uses very few words now, mostly yes or no or "hmmm" for when she doesn't know the answer to what you're asking or how to perform a task you may be asking her to do. She requires much more guidance than in the past and that takes patience. She now requires specific instructions for example on how to sit in a car, so trying to get her into my car was very difficult. It was so difficult that at one point I cried after I dropped her off because it was horrible watching her trying to follow my instructions on how to move her feet and turn her legs to get into the passenger seat. It was one of the most frustrating things we've been through in a long time. On the plus side, she still has a great appetite, and still loves sweets. As of late she's started to lose weight as well, but we're not sure of the cause.

Something I thought would take a lot of patience, hasn't taken any. Mom has been in Depends full time since 2015. I can change her with ease, and I take her "Mom bag" with fidget toys, magazines, extra Depends, wipes and clothes wherever we go.

One of the most interesting things that occurred was that Mom began reading everything out loud in early 2014, which continued until February 2016 right around her birthday. During the time that she read out loud, we were unable to take her word search puzzles or her favorite Reader's Digest with us into the doctor's offices or other locations because it would be too distracting for others. Hearing her read every word out loud in her loud and monotone voice is unnerving in a way. She would read any and every thing, such as signs inside elevators, traffic signs and license plates, and words on the food and drugs we purchased. Needless to say we got some strange looks in the grocery store or pharmacy. Imagine coming down the aisle and hearing someone say out loud "Kaopectate for Diarrhea". People would hurry down the aisles to get away from us. The neurologist didn't seem concerned about Mom reading out loud at all, and said that it would eventually stop just as it started. And it did. She can still read, but now reads to herself again. I'm guessing that shoppers everywhere are relieved!

Patience is more important than ever as this disease progresses.

HEARTBREAK

There's been a lot of heartbreak since the book was published. My beloved Aunt Frances Beard (Frannie) died in August 2013 – it was one of the toughest losses for me as she was, as I said in her eulogy, my "go to girl". Frannie was the best listener ever, and she loved how I cared for Mom. I always ran everything by her and she was the perfect substitute for Mom's great wisdom. I miss her terribly but she'd be very proud of me.

We all know it's coming, but when your loved one no longer remembers you it is the most heartbreaking thing ever. October 2013 was the very first time Mom didn't remember my name, but she knew I was her daughter. I prayed it was just a one-time thing but knew that it wasn't. I didn't overreact but I drove home as fast as I could, and then cried when I got there. But the worst heartbreaking event occurred on my 55th birthday on January 3, 2014. I headed to Mom's group home with a cake and a gallon of ice cream. Fellow resident Mr. Broadus was playing happy birthday to me on his harmonica. I wanted to have a nice party at Mom's group home so not to risk having her out past the "sundowning hour" when her anxiety level rises off the charts. But the party turned out to be a very bad idea. Mom's confusion didn't allow her to recognize whose birthday it was. She was so frustrated, she started to cry and pushed her slice of cake on the floor. It was heartbreaking to see her so upset. I cleaned up the cake and quickly headed home. I cried and cried when I got home, then tried to have fun with Tim. We went to an amazing restaurant and it was wonderful, but in the back of my mind I was still focused on the fact that Mom may never remember me again.

The other amazing thing about this disease is that Mom's totally forgotten that she was ever married, or that she had two kids, so my dad and sister's existence are gone from Mom's memory forever. Though she loves photos, the photos of my father, sister or my niece do nothing to jog her recollection of them. When she sees me, she has recognition that I'm familiar to her, and that's ok with me.

In April 2015 using Depends came into our lives permanently. I was prepared to give her "the talk" about wearing Depends but didn't have to. At least that wasn't as heartbreaking as it could have been. I just explained that the Depends were going to be her new underwear that she can always depend on if she has an accident. She said to me "I Depend on you too". It was priceless, as are many of the things she says.

One on the worst things that happened since the book was published was losing our beloved Dr. Coerver to Denver, Colorado. I'm so happy for her that she found new opportunities, but wished it could have happened in D.C. so she could continue to be Mom's doctor. When I found out she was leaving, my heart skipped a few beats. I wondered what would happen to Mom now. While she doesn't need much help in terms of medicine, Mom was very connected to Dr. Coerver and I doubt that we'll ever find that again. We had one last visit together and Mom and Dr. Coerver had a great time, even taking a few pictures together. Dr. Coerver encouraged me to continue to use the practice and the new woman who'd be joining the neurology team. I may do that eventually, but want to first see if I can find an acceptable neurologist closer to home. So far it isn't looking good.

By far the greatest heartbreak for me was losing my beloved Tim in July of 2016. My husband and soulmate died suddenly after a series of strokes while we were on vacation in NY. We were living our retirement dream of traveling in our RV and working in exchange for free camping (called workamping) when that dream was derailed. Being Tim's caregiver for the 6 days he was in the hospital in Cooperstown, NY was simultaneously heartbreaking and an honor. I remember how much love and care Tim provided to me when I was so sick for almost 13 years in the first half of our marriage. I can't even count the amount of time he spent at the hospital with me. I'm thankful that Tim died pain-free and not knowing that his strokes were actually caused by stage 4 pancreatic cancer. In an odd way, I consider his fairly-quick death to be a blessing, because I don't know anyone who would want their loved one to suffer for months before their deaths. Pancreatic cancer is nothing but suffering, and you die anyway. I'm glad God allowed Tim to think he was back at our majestic campsite and simply go to sleep. It's definitely what Tim would have wanted. Now it's up to me to carry on with our dream in a slightly different way in addition to continuing to care for Mom. It's impossible to adequately explain how much Tim helped me with Mom. He'd pick Mom up from the group home and drive her to the doctor, and I'd leave work and meet them at the doctor's office. It saved me from having to take more time off from work. He also picked up her prescriptions, visited Mom while I was traveling, and even did small errands at the group home. He supported me through the toughest days of mom's disease and held me as I cried on many days. Of the more than 200 speaking engagements I've done since the book was published, Tim attended more than half of them. So many of my friends from the Alzheimer's Association were devastated by Tim's death because they had gotten to know him so well on the many occasions we were all together. He loved being in the fight against Alzheimer's disease with me, and I believe that he was even more devastated than I was the first time Mom didn't recognize him. When my sister died in 2011 I chose not to tell my Mom. So five years later when Tim died on the same day my sister did, I kept that to myself as well. I'm still very surprised that Mom outlived Tim. Through my heartbreak, I'll continue to care for Mom as if Tim's still here with me.

PREPARATION

I'm happy to report that Mom is still at the group home called Mamie's Loving Care, where she has been since October 2009. Though the cost of her care is very reasonable, I have to add to her retirement funds to pay for her monthly costs. I've recently filled out subsidy program paperwork to determine if I can get additional funds for Mom. In the three years since the book was released, nothing has changed at Mamie's Loving Care. They still provide the best care ever, and love Mom as much as I do.

As much as I love Mamie's Loving Care I've researched other group homes in my area to be prepared in the event Ms. Mamie decides to retire at some point soon. At the request of my estate lawyer, I asked Ms. Mamie if she had a succession plan for her business, and she shared that her son would run the business in her absence.

I'm still working as a Government contractor, which I began in September of 2012. While I haven't saved as much as I intended, it's currently very easy to supplement Mom's funds.

One of the most important elements of being prepared is to make life simpler. Once Mom required Depends full time, I arranged for the monthly delivery of disposable underwear, wipes, and liners. Having the products delivered right to the door is the true essence of simple. I can add to or change my order prior to delivery each month. It's important to try to be one step ahead of whatever may come next. I use a company called Disposables Delivered and I simply love them!

There are many effective tools available that can help us be prepared for most any situation. Near the end of 2013, I began researching cell phone applications (APPs) and reviewing their functionality and usefulness for caregivers. One of the things I was looking for was something to track Mom's care and appointments. I found more than I had ever bargained for and began using a variety of APPs.

One of my favorites APPs is called **Senior Care**, by the Institute on Aging which tracks all appointments Mom has and the meds she takes and notifies any others I want to designate to receive the information. I also love **Music First**, by Coro Health. It plays songs designed just for Alzheimer's patients. When I turn it on, Mom's anxiety lessens immediately. There's even a playlist specifically for "sundowners", a condition that impacts some dementia patients in the evening and changes their behavior and anxiety levels. My other favorite is the APP called the **Alzheimer's and Dementia Companion** by Home Instead Senior Care. It's a resource that includes tips for caregivers by caregivers. It's divided into twenty-five categories, such as anger, hygiene, bedtime struggles, holidays, and medication. It answers questions such as "what do I do when my loved one refuses to bathe?" And "how do I handle Dad's angry outbursts?" There are lots of answers to choose from and a variety of suggestions to try with your loved one, which is very comforting. An APP called **Lifetimes Talk** by The Game of Reminiscence Inc. is a game with the purpose of starting conversations between loved ones and friends who visit dementia patients. It has topics such as Favorite Recipes, First Dates, School Memories etc. I love that it potentially gets people visiting and talking again because so many people stop visiting once dementia enters our lives.

I also love a few general caregivers APPs. One is called **Caregiver Prayer** which offers a beautiful photo and a bible-based prayer for each day accompanied by a short lesson. It's an APP that has been very helpful to me. I also love an APP called **The Now!** It's a daily collection of quotes and inspiration to soothe the caregiver's soul. I look forward to reading the daily messages because they are simultaneously comforting and thought-provoking. Because stress can be a huge problem for caregivers, I rely on three APPs to help keep my stress levels down. One is a Meditation APP called **Mindfulness**. It has great programs to help us focus on ourselves and remain calm. Another is an APP called **Relax Melodies** that allows you to add different elements to make your own spa music. The elements include piano, flute, river, ocean, and winds. The resulting tunes are very relaxing. The last APP that I find very useful and enjoyable is a digital "coloring book" called **Recolor** that you operate using finger taps to select colors and fill in open spaces. I'm not a game APP person, but this coloring book APP is amazingly relaxing. If you believe that an APP can help you with any caregiver or dementia need, simply search in your APP store to see what's available to make your life easier and less stressful.

Preparation is a key to making great memories. We need to think about everything we may need before venturing out for a fun time. I was researching a new location for church retreats and wanted to take Mom with me on the ride. It was almost two hours from the group home. I timed it so that I'd have Mom home before her early afternoon dinner and her sundowners set in. The trip was very pleasant and she had a great time! My preparation included snacks and fidget toys for the car, songs we could sing along to, and photo books and magazines she could look through on the trip, stops for the rest room and lunch. Mom loved the mountains and the beauty of the retreat center.

One of the obvious things I hadn't prepared for was losing Tim. I never thought I'd need a backup plan for him. Thankfully, I received an offer from Jan Lipscomb my great friend from church to help me with Mom when I need it. She's the perfect person too, because she works with kids with disabilities and is one of the most compassionate people I know. As devastated as I am about Tim's death, I do take solace in the fact that I'll have help when I need it. Jan met me at Mom's and the three of us had a great visit. I know that if Jan needs to be with Mom to help out while I'm traveling, Mom's in fabulous hands. After Jan and I set up our plan, I also received an offer from Yvonne Upshaw, another great friend to help out with Mom too. I'm thrilled that I have a plan and a backup for Mom!

I also want to be prepared as possible for when I need help myself. I met with an Elder Care and an Estate attorney, introduced to me by my financial planner. I finished preparing all of the legal documents for my estate and for Mom's care if something were to happen to me. Being prepared is critical, even when it comes to the things you don't want to prepare for!

HUMOR

Mom still has an awesome sense of humor...Here are just a few examples.

I had taken Mom a cake my daughter Kim made, as I was leaving, she asked "Are you leaving?" When I said yes, she said "OK, you can go, but leave the cake". I always come in second to the sweets!

Mom may seem like she isn't paying attention, but that blank stare on her face can sometimes be deceiving! On one recent drive, Mom asked "Did you see that Stop sign? You didn't stop!" I promised her that I'd stop next time, to which she replied "please do"!

I was trying (in vain of course) to explain to Mom about my blog called "Conquering Life". Many of the posts are about her. Mom's comment about my explanation was "a blog doesn't sound like it's anything good!" Thanks Mom!

When shown the 2015 Easter photo of herself, me, Kim and Kendal, Mom replied "This is a great photo of me. Who are those other people in my picture? They look nice, are they?" I assured her we are really nice people.

As we drove home from a doctor's appointment Mom asked if we could stop for ice cream. Her reasoning was simple. She said "since I had to endure all the poking and prodding, I deserve ice cream!" Ok Mom, great point we will stop for ice cream!

HOPE

The greatest hope to end this disease lies with the UsAgainstAlzheimer's organization. It's a powerful advocacy group that I'm very proud to be involved with. UsAgainstAlzheimer's was founded by George and Trish Vradenburg and they've worked tirelessly to find a cure for Alzheimer's. Each year there's a National Alzheimer's Summit and Hill Day in Washington DC and it includes an Out of the Shadows fundraising dinner. I have participated in two Summits, which includes an all-day session of presentations and panel discussions. I've loved working with Ginny Biggar, the Executive Director for Patient-Caregiver, Faith and Senior Living Intiatives for UsAgainstAlzheimer's. In September 2016 I was honored to participate in one of the panels entitled, "Voices of Alzheimer's: Engaging Individuals Living with Dementia and Caregivers on the Path to a Cure". As part of the panel, I shared some of the joys and challenges of caring for Mom. I was asked by the panel's moderator, Meryl Comer to explain the greatest challenge of caring for Mom after Tim's sudden death. My answer was that it's going to be hardest to replace all of the little things Tim did for Mom, like visiting her if I was working, picking up supplies or driving her around for errands and lunch, all of which he loved to do. He loved Mom as much as I do. As shocking and heartbreaking as Tim's death was, I still have to focus enough to care for Mom.

On the second day of the Summit, participants travel to Capitol Hill to meet with members of Congress to encourage them to vote on Alzheimer's related legislation and to request additional funding for Alzheimer's research. Meeting with members of Congress or their staffers makes me feel as if I'm fighting against this disease with thousands of others. One year as part of those Congressional meetings, we shared our loved ones through memorabilia in Shadow Boxes that each of us made. It was a very emotional experience for us and I believe our stories had a great impact on the Senators and Representatives we met with!

In addition to the Summit, there is also an UsAgainstAlzheimer's Community Support Group on Facebook which has more than 4,800 members from around the world. I'm proud to be one of four co-moderators of the group and have been very active on the page since 2013, answering questions, posting articles and information and providing comfort and support to our members. It's one of the most rewarding endeavors I've been involved with. I even had the pleasure of meeting some of the current and former co-moderators of the UsAgainstAlzheimer's group, especially my friend Ann Napoletan. We will all be in this fight until a cure for this horrible disease is found. I'm proud to have donated a portion of all of my book earnings to Alzheimer's research.

After Tim's death I spent a couple of days saying to myself, what in the world am I going to do? I knew I had to do a few things quickly, including getting rid of my favorite Cadillac CTS, and getting something more practical to drive Mom and Kendal. I did both of those things and in the process learned that I can accomplish anything, even in grief! My church friends at St. Mark's Episcopal Church-Capitol Hill organized a small support group to help me through the tough times and we meet once a month. I'm beyond grateful to Jan and Don Lipscomb, Louise Walsh, Tracy Councill, Charmian Crawford, Erika Lehman, Yvonne Upshaw, and Ozgur and Lisa Ozkan for being there when I need them.

Grief is a daily process, and you have to take one day at a time. When someone in your life has dementia, you're already grieving for them, and the person they used to be even though they are still alive. It's a slow kind of death. Right now, in late December of 2016, I'm dealing with two types of grief, one for my Mom who is still with me, and my husband who isn't.

The great news is, I have lots of hope for the future. Hope that my Mom will remain fairly stable for the time being, and hope that within the next couple of years, a cure will be found for this horrible disease. I also have hope that I will continue to carry out all of the promises I made to my husband Tim, namely to remain vigilant in the fight to find a cure for Alzheimer's, to continue to share our story with as many people as possible and on the personal side to continue to tour the country in our RV experiencing as many adventures as possible.

My mission and the primary focus of this book is to "Focus on the Memories" that each of us make. I hope you enjoy our memories!

Introduction

Mom was very aware after her 2006 diagnosis that she had dementia, and as her condition worsened she used to always say "I don't know what I'm doing!" in the most exasperated voice you can imagine. It always hurt me to my core when she'd say that and it spurred me to continue doing whatever I can to help find a cure for this dreaded disease. As mom's condition worsened I needed inspiration on many days!

Over the years, I've been inspired by many of the photos Tim and I have taken on our travels and began writing inspirational quotes to accompany some of my favorite photos and saved them to look at when I was having a bad day. The photos really perked mom up too, and she'd say "wow" upon seeing many of the scenic views. She was amazed that Tim and I had traveled to so many places and taken all the photos ourselves. Because we loved the photos so much, I decided to publish them in a book in the hopes that they might be uplifting for others. In honor of my mom, there's no rhyme or reason or specific order to the photos, just as there's no order in mom's brain because of her dementia.

No matter who you are caring for or what disease they have, I hope our photos and quotes in this book help to refresh your spirit!

You can conquer any situation when you have great support!

Watching the sun rise can change both
the landscape and your mindset.

Grand Canyon National Park, Arizona © Tim Veney, 2016

Engage your active imagination! You may even see an ice cream cone in the desert.

Red Rock Canyon, Nevada © Loretta Woodward Veney, 2016

When you view life from a positive perspective
your problems are more manageable!

Mt. Rigi, Switzerland © Tim Veney, 2016

Surround yourself with people who support you no matter which way the wind blows!

Copenhagen, Denmark © Tim Veney, 2016

It takes a village to overcome mountainous obstacles!
Know who in your village can be of help to you!

Jungfrau, Switzerland © Tim Veney, 2016

Mt. Rigi, Switzerland © Tim Veney, 2016

Climbing to the top is worth all the effort!

Tuscany, Italy © Loretta Woodward Veney, 2016

Spending time on a body of
water can make you feel grand!

Grand Canal Venice, Italy © Loretta Woodward Veney, 2016

Even if things look bleak
better times are right around the corner!

Santorini, Greece © Loretta Woodward Veney, 2016

Porto Santo Stefano, Italy © Tim Veney, 2016

Grab a lifeline when you need one!

Cancun, Mexico © Loretta Woodward Veney, 2016

Mt. Rainier National Park, Washington © Loretta Woodward Veney, 2016

Stand tall even if things begin to crumble around you!

Ephesus, Turkey © Loretta Woodward Veney, 2016

Go to your place of solitude often
even if it's only in your mind!

Tuscany, Italy © Loretta Woodward Veney, 2016

Lucerne, Switzerland © Loretta Woodward Veney, 2016

Steer carefully to avoid debris
that could throw you off your path!

Glacier Bay National Park, Alaska © Tim Veney, 2016

Driving can be freeing, even if you have no idea where you're headed!

Tuscany, Italy © Loretta Woodward Veney, 2016

Lucerne, Switzerland © Tim Veney, 2016

When the world feels as cold as ice, sip a warm drink!

Glacier Bay National Park, Alaska © Loretta Woodward Veney, 2016

When advocating
for loved ones be
a giant force!

Abu Simbel, Egypt © Loretta Woodward Veney, 2016

Santorini, Greece © Tim Veney, 2016

Every step you take brings you closer to success!

Chichen Itza, Mexico © Tim Veney, 2016

Prickly situations require
immediate solutions.

Scottsdale, Arizona © Loretta Woodward Veney, 2016

Barbados, Lesser Antilles © Tim Veney, 2016

Your faith holds your foundation together even if a few pieces of you fall apart.

Glacier Bay National Park, Alaska © Tim Veney, 2016

The sun brings out the
beauty and majesty of life!

Aswan, Egypt on the River Nile © Loretta Woodward Veney, 2016

You can conquer anything
when you stand strong!

Luxor, Egypt © Loretta Woodward Veney, 2016

Bright colors uplift your spirits!

Copenhagen, Denmark © Tim Veney, 2016

Corfu, Greece © Tim Veney, 2016

Tulum, Mexico © Loretta Woodward Veney, 2016

Find inspirations that make
you want to jump for joy!

Milan, Italy © Loretta Woodward Veney, 2016

Patience and preparation make
it easier to reach the pinnacle!

Grand Canyon National Park West Rim, Arizona © Tim Veney, 2016

St. Thomas, U.S. Virgin Islands © Loretta Woodward Veney, 2016

May your life reflect everything positive about you!

Maple Valley, Washington © Loretta Woodward Veney, 2016

Gather your strength to cross life's bridges!

Mt. Rainier National Park, Washington © Loretta Woodward Veney, 2016

Rhodes, Greece © Tim Veney, 2016

Take a seat to take care of you!

Maui, Hawaii © Loretta Woodward Veney, 2016

Mt. Rainier National Park, Washington © Tim Veney, 2016

Cancun, Mexico © Loretta Woodward Veney, 2016

Shafer Trail in Moab, Utah © Loretta Woodward Veney, 2016

Charge your battery naturally
with a beautiful view!

Porto Santo Stefano, Italy © Loretta Woodward Veney, 2016

Taking great care of everything you love can have amazing results!

Siena, Italy © Tim Veney, 2016

Slow down so life's frenetic pace
doesn't overtake you like rushing water!

Snoqualmie Falls, Washington © Loretta Woodward Veney, 2016

Madrid, Spain © Tim Veney, 2016

Getting off the beaten path can
lead to beautiful discoveries!

Maui, Hawaii © Loretta Woodward Veney, 2016

Antelope Canyon, Arizona © Tim Veney, 2016

Cherish life's peaks and calm waters and you'll be better prepared when things change.

Skagway, Alaska © Loreta Woodward Veney, 2016

There's more than one
way to get up a hill!

Zurich, Switzerland © Tim Veney, 2016

When there is even a glimmer of light, there's hope!

Samana, Dominican Republic © Loretta Veney, 2016

Dubai, United Arab Emirates © Tim Veney, 2016

The higher you have to climb, the stronger you get!

Eze, France © Tim Veney, 2016

Copenhagen, Denmark © Tim Veney, 2016

You see everything more clearly when your spirits are high!

Junfrau, Switzerland © Tim Veney, 2016

Call a friend when you need a lift!

Grand Canyon National Park, Arizona © Tim Veney 2016

Sometimes we forget that we aren't alone in this world!

Chicago, Illinois © Tim Veney, 2016

Even a few minutes alone can be restorative!

Grand canal, Venice, Italy © Loretta Woodward Veney, 2016

Leave no stone unturned
until you have what you need!

Kodachrome Basin, Utah © Loretta Woodward Veney, 2016

When a path isn't readily available create your own!

Vancouver, Canada © Loretta Woodward Veney, 2016

From a lofty perch, you can behold the world!

Lucerne, Switzerland © Loretta Woodward Veney, 2016

Look for the beauty and worth in everything and everyone!

Coronado, California © Loretta Woodward Veney, 2016

Even the rain
can be tranquil!

Maui, Hawaii © Tim Veney, 2016

Leave all your worries in your special place!

Martha's Vineyard, Massachusetts © Loretta Veney Woodward, 2016

Magnificent places boost your spirits!

Yosemite National Park, California © Tim Veney, 2016

Mykonos, Greece © Tim Veney, 2016

Chicago, Illinois © Tim Veney, 2016

With the right resources your challenges sail away!

Porto Santo Stefano, Italy © Tim Veney, 2016

Sometimes we need a little direction!

Martha's Vineyard, Massachusetts © Loretta Woodward Veney, 2016

A little time away can bring a lot of solitude!

Xcaret, Mexico © Loretta Woodward Veney, 2016

Some days you feel like you're falling off a ledge, but at the end of the day you'll still be standing!

Grand Canyon National Park West Rim, Arizona © Tim Veney, 2016

Being close to a force of nature helps you to feel your own power!

Niagara Falls, Canada © Tim Veney, 2016

Luxor, Egypt © Tim Veney, 2016

Keep looking until you see the big picture!

Copenhagen, Denmark © Loretta Woodward Veney, 2016

Storms may be scary but they always pass!

Moab, Utah © Tim Veney, 2016

Let everyone
see your
shining light!

Paris, France © Loretta Woodward Veney, 2016

Don't look back, the strong support behind you will hold you up!

Cairo, Egypt © Loretta Woodward Veney, 2016

Pastry shop, Lucca, Italy © Tim Veney, 2016

Sunrise at Abu Simbel, Egypt © Tim Veney, 2016

Life is tougher without the right pillars in your life!

Athens, Greece © Tim Veney, 2016

Take a quick break to do something fun!

Herkimer, New York © Loretta Woodward Veney, 2016

Exploring different places to dine and shop brings new excitement!

Eze, France © Loretta Woodward Veney, 2016

Get out of the house, you may discover hidden gems!

Nice, France © Loretta Woodward Veney, 2016

Glacier Bay National Park, Alaska © Loretta Woodward Veney, 2016

When you're at your wits end, imagine having a beach all to yourself!

St. Croix, U.S. Virgin Islands © Loretta Woodward Veney, 2016

You're in charge of your own palace,
don't let others overrule you!

Monaco, France © Tim Veney, 2016

Take life one step at a time
so you don't slip and fall!

Mendenhall Glacier, Alaska © Loretta Woodward Veney, 2016

Encourage the negative people in your life to fly away!

Dubai, United Arab Emirates © Loretta Woodward Veney, 2016

Bryce Canyon, Utah © Loretta Woodward Veney, 2016

Niagara Falls, Canada © Tim Veney, 2016

Not every path is straight and narrow, it's the curved paths that help you grow.

Antelope Canyon, Arizona © Tim Veney, 2016

Having great relationships includes building bridges with loved ones.

Natural Bridge, Virginia © Loretta Woodward Veney, 2016

Some days can be a real bear, but
trust that the situation will improve!

Skyline Drive, Virginia © Loretta Woodward Veney, 2016

Beautiful skies tell a very spiritual story!

La Jolla, California © Tim Veney, 2016

Moments are more precious when you're not watching the clock!

Prague, Czech Republic © Loretta Woodward Veney, 2016

Road to Bryce Canyon, Utah © Loretta Woodward Veney, 2016

It's ok to lean a little when you don't feel like standing up straight!

Pisa, Italy © Loretta Woodward Veney, 2016

Caring for yourself first ensures continued growth!

Butchart Gardens, Victoria British Columbia, Canada © Tim Veney, 2016

Don't go off in too many directions
or you may end up all wet!

Seattle, Washington © Tim Veney, 2016

A sanctuary is wherever you feel peace!

Shrine Mont, Orkney Springs, Virginia © Loretta Woodward Veney, 2016

Toledo, Spain © Loretta Woodward Veney, 2016

When someone is down, lift them up!

Salzburg, Austria © Tim Veney, 2016

Your spirit can soar when you take a retreat!

Jungfrau, Switzerland © Tim Veney, 2016

Not even a huge barrier should crush your spirit.

Arches National Park, Utah © Tim Veney, 2016

Cancun, Mexico © Loretta Woodward Veney, 2016

Wisdom is the result of years of growth!

Mt. Rainier National Park, Washington © Loretta Woodward Veney, 2016

Opening
closed
doors
may
reveal
the
answers
you
need!

Madrid, Spain © Tim Veney, 2016

Make your home your sanctuary!

Maple Valley, Washington © Tim Veney, 2016

La Jolla, California © Loretta Woodward Veney, 2016

Clevedale Historic Inn and Gardens, Spartanburg, South Carolina © Loretta Woodward Veney, 2016

What you believe you're experiencing
may only be an illusion!

Vancouver, Canada © Loretta Woodward Veney, 2016

Don't be so preoccupied that you miss
the beautiful things in this world!

Butchart Gardens, Victoria British Columbia, Canada © Tim Veney, 2016

What makes you magnificent is
the fact that you're different!

Hot air balloon ride, Dubai, United Arab Emirates © Tim Veney, 2016

Believe that you are a mighty fortress!

San Juan, Puerto Rico © Loretta Woodward Veney, 2016

Life is short don't let that ship sail without you!

St. Thomas, U.S. Virgin Islands © Loretta Woodward Veney, 2016

Find an energizing outlet so stress doesn't box you in!

Aswan, Egypt © Tim Veney, 2016

Arches National Park, Utah © Loretta Woodward Veney, 2016

Make a wish, it may just come true!

Trevi Fountain, Rome, Italy © Tim Veney, 2016

You're surrounded by a wall of love!

Valley of the Kings, Luxor, Egypt © Tim Veney, 2016

Discover the
sheer joy of
being outdoors!

Road to Hana, Maui, Hawaii © Tim Veney, 2016

To really understand a situation, examine it closely!

Scottsdale, Arizona © Loretta Woodward Veney, 2016

Just because the handwriting is on the wall doesn't mean life is over!

Kom Ombo, Egypt © Tim Veney

Mt. Rainier National Park, Washington © Tim Veney, 2016

Find that special jolt of energy you need!

St. Thomas, U.S. Virgin Islands © Tim Veney, 2016

When you fit all
the right pieces
together you'll
be unstoppable!

Burj Khalifa in Dubai, United Arab Emirates © Tim Veney, 2016

The three greatest pillars of support
are your family, friends and faith!

Pyramids in Cairo, Egypt © Tim Veney, 2016

Let a beautiful environment engulf you!

Herkimer, New York © Loretta Woodward Veney, 2016

Stay calm and work to get to the root of the problem!

Yosemite National Park, California © Loretta Woodward Veney, 2016

Gelato shop Siena, Italy © Loretta Woodward Veney, 2016

On the toughest days, even a small accomplishment can be a triumph!

Arc de Triomphe, Paris © Loretta Woodward Veney, 2016

Seize the energy each seasonal change brings!

Shenandoah National Park, Virginia © Tim Veney, 2016

When you dance with your
friends, your stress disappears!

Luau in Maui, Hawaii © Tim Veney, 2016

If you're buried under stress, find the resources needed to dig yourself out!

Clinton, Maryland © Loretta Woodward Veney, 2016

You never outgrow playing in a treehouse!

Herkimer, New York © Loretta Woodward Veney, 2016

Self-care includes enjoying new explorations!

Maui, Hawaii © Tim Veney, 2016

National Harbor's ICE, Washington, D.C. © Tim Veney, 2016

Seek out places that fill you with the spirit!

The Vatican, Rome, Italy © Loretta Woodward Veney, 2016

Antelope Canyon, Arizona © Tim Veney, 2016

Porto Santo Stefano, Italy © Tim Veney, 2016

Epilogue

As I look back on all the travel and camping adventures Tim and I experienced in our almost 31 years of marriage, I'm so grateful for both the memories we made and the amazing photos we took to preserve them.

Cherish your family memories!

Contact Information

Want to book Loretta for a speaking engagement?

Loretta Woodward Veney

www.lorettaveney.com

lwveney@lorettaveney.com